Number
TRACING

Page Color Test

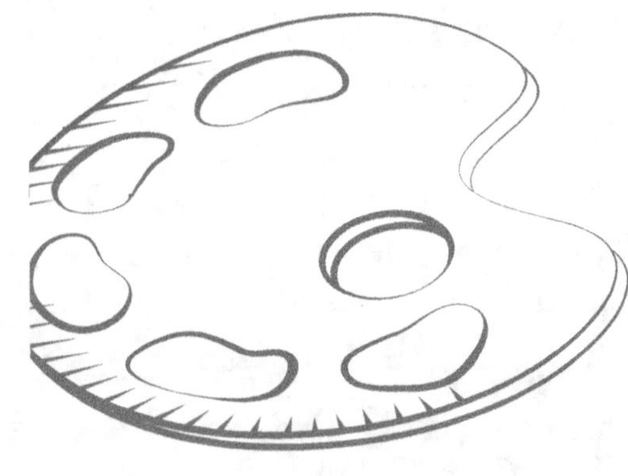

Let's Start warming Up:

Trace the Number 0

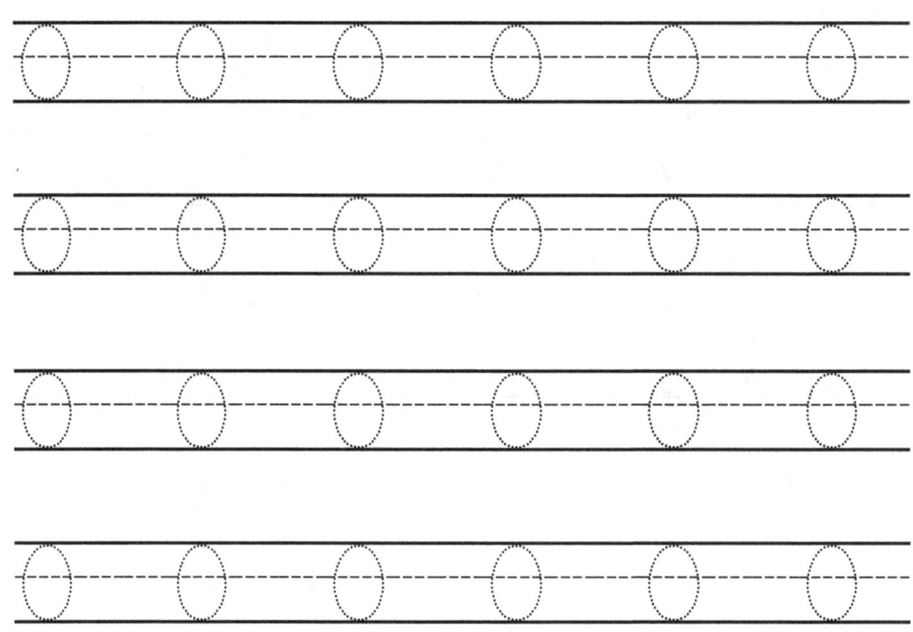

Trace the word Zero

Trace the Number 1

Trace the word One

1

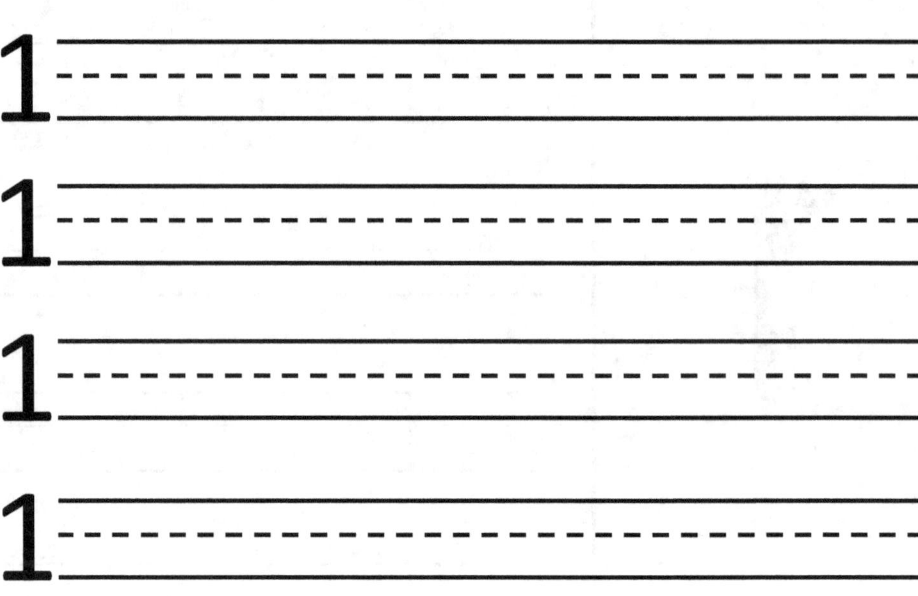

Color One Orange

One

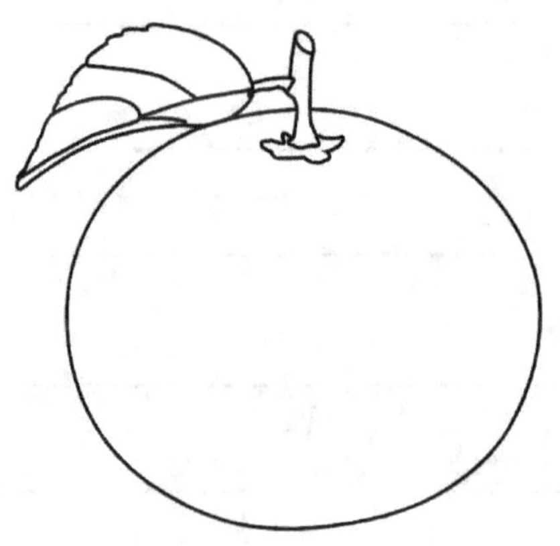
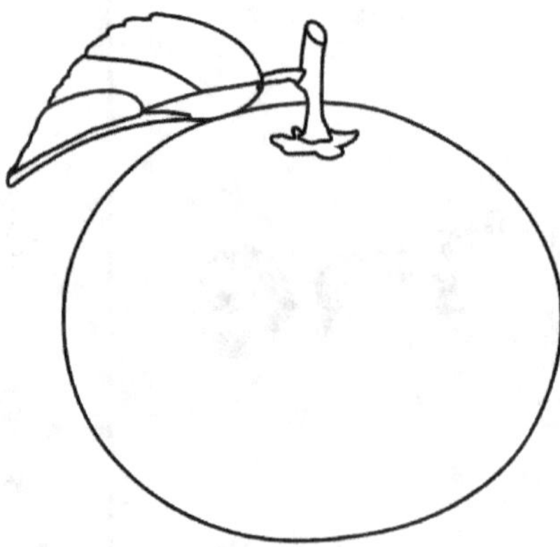

2

Trace the Number 2

Two

Trace the word Two

2

Write Number 2

2 2
2 2
2 2
2 2

Two

Color Two Apples

3

Trace the Number 3

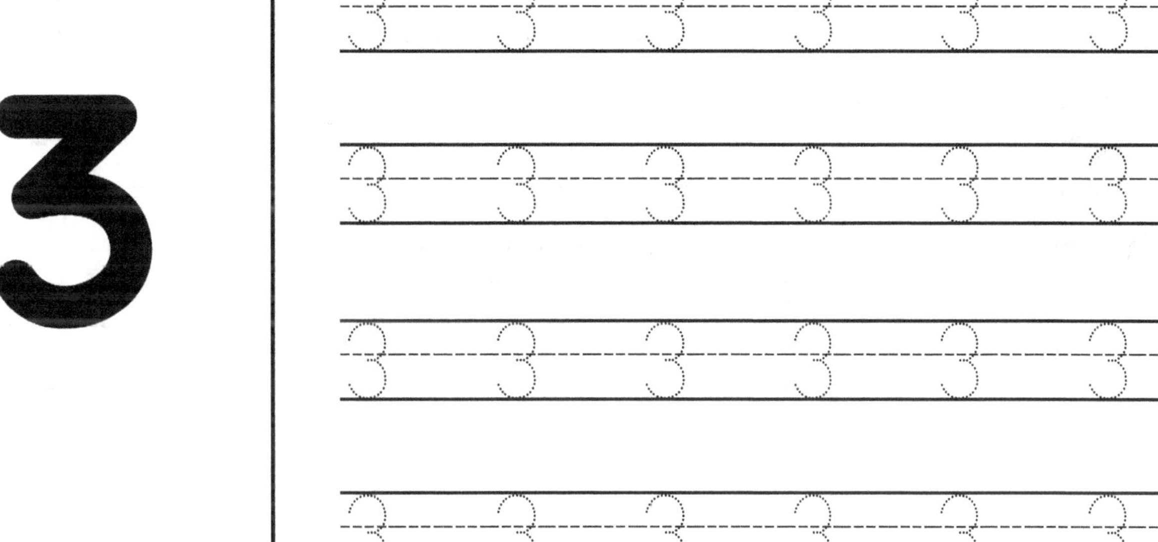

Three

Trace the word Three

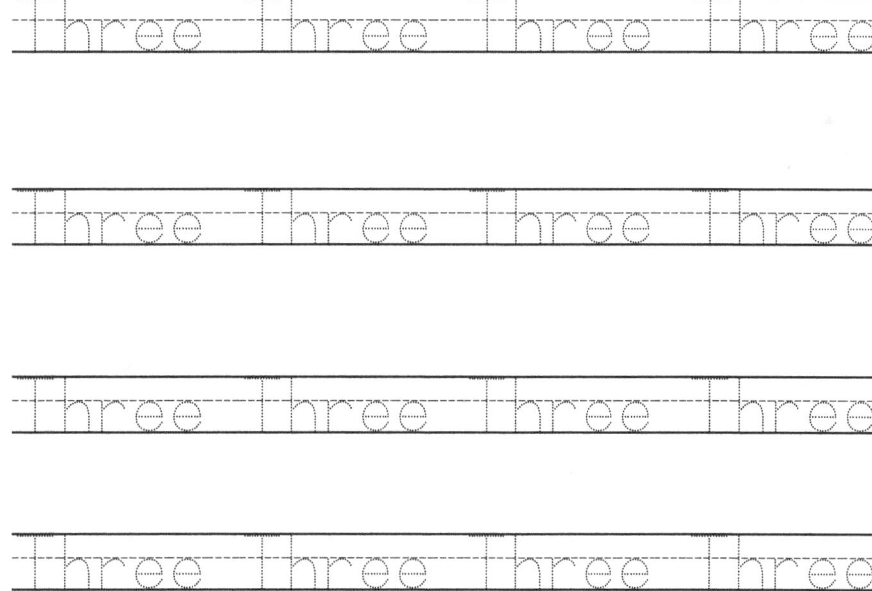

Write Number 3

3
3
3
3

3

Three

Color Three Pears

Trace the Number 4

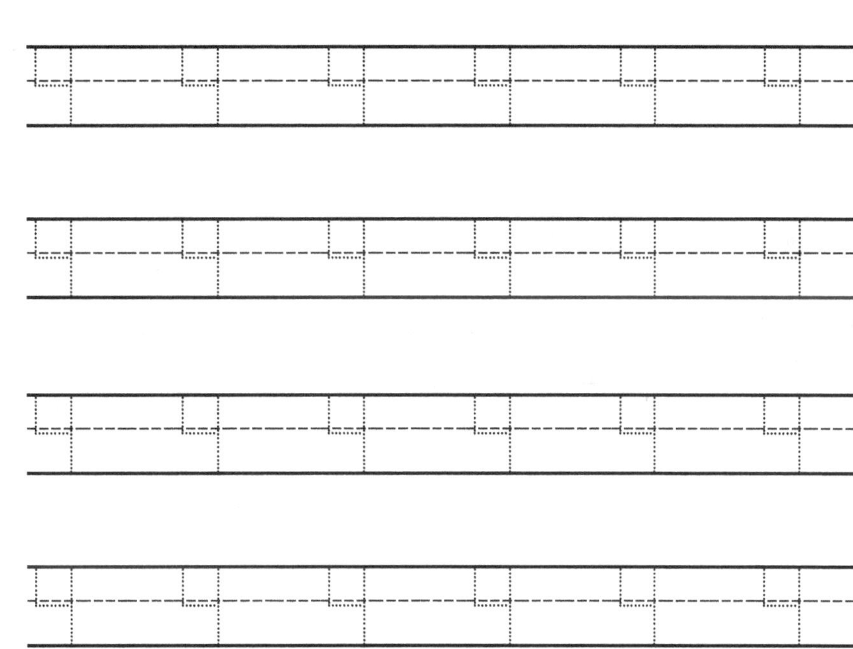

Trace the word Four

4

Write Number 4

4
4
4
4

Four

Color Four water Melon slices

5

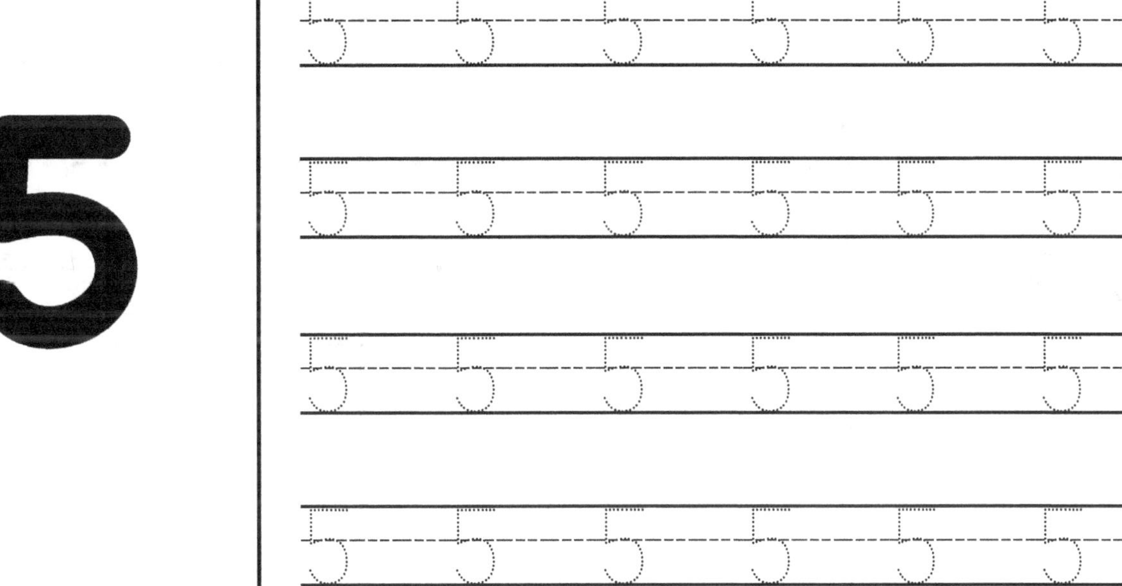

Five

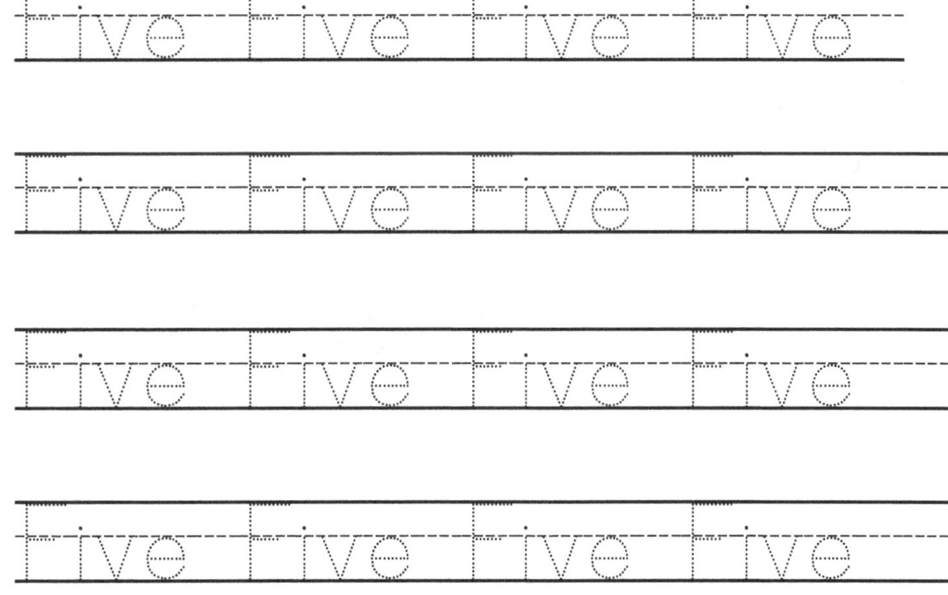

5

Write Number 5

5 ─────────────────
5 ─────────────────
5 ─────────────────
5 ─────────────────

Color Five Tomatoes

Five

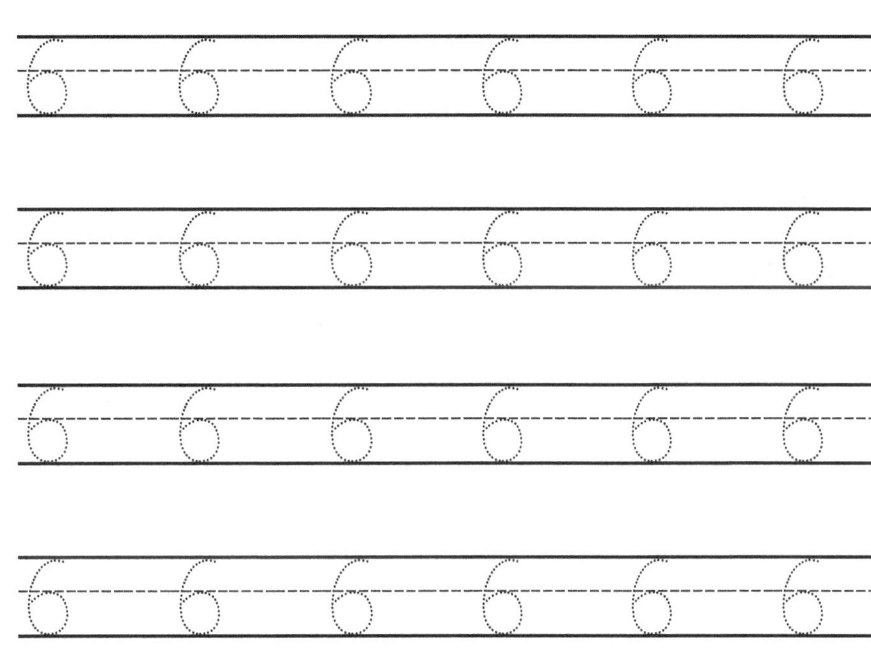

Trace the Number 6

Trace the word Six

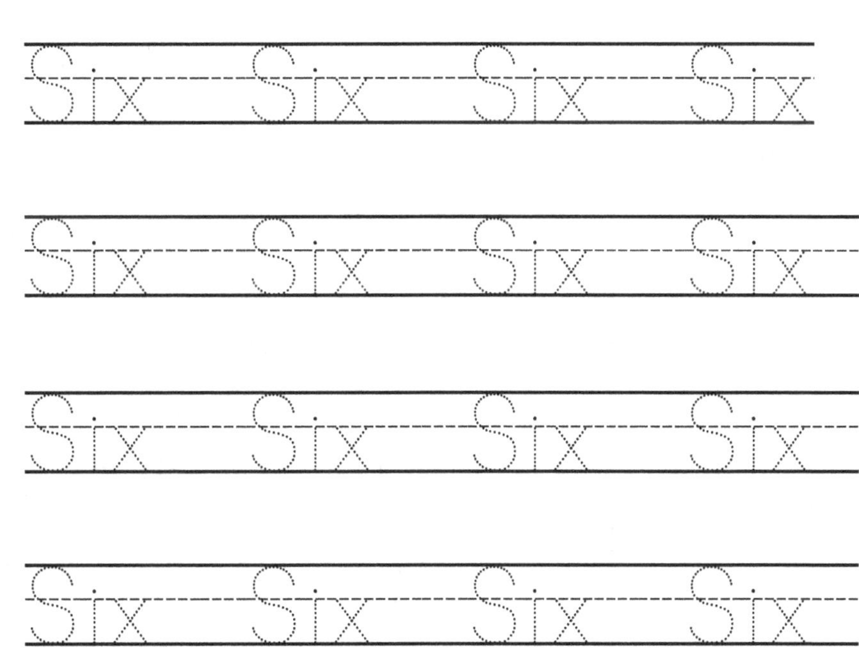

6

Write Number 6

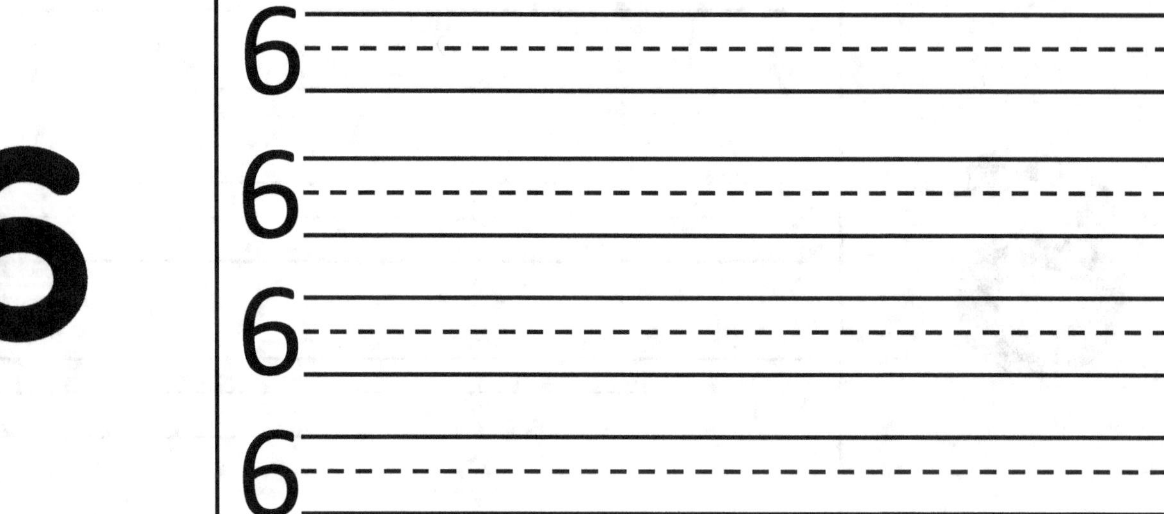

6 6 6 6

Six

Color Six Carrots

Trace the Number 7

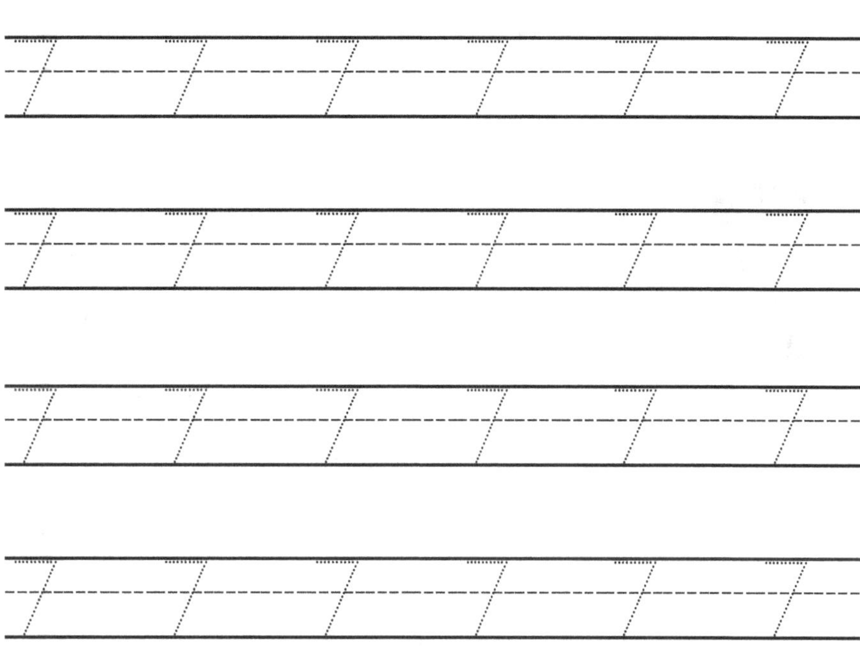

Trace the word Seven

Write Number 7

7
7
7
7

Seven

Color Seven Pumpkins

Trace the Number 8

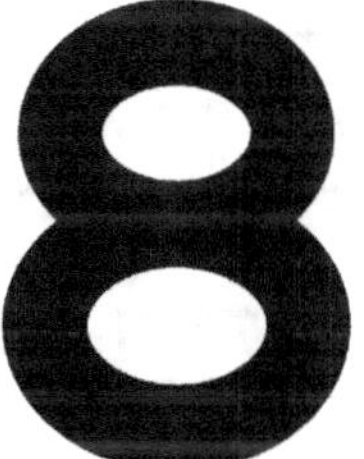

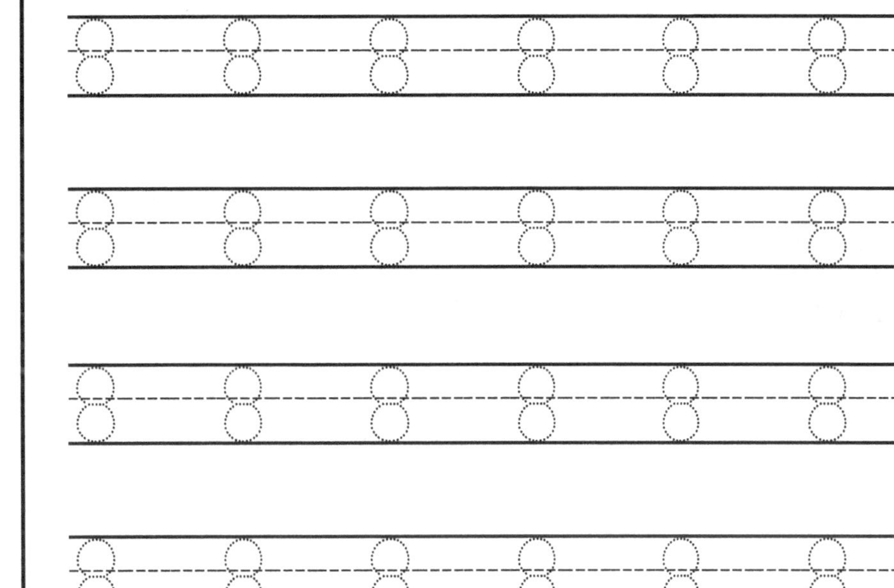

Trace the word Eight

8

Write Number 8

8
8
8
8

Eight

Color Eight Strawberries

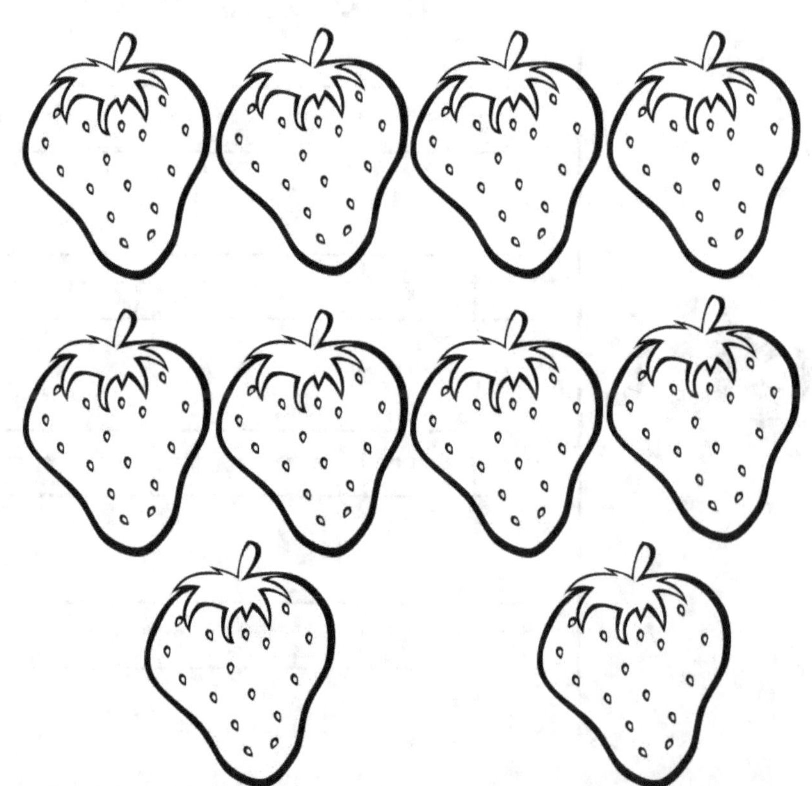

Trace the Number 9

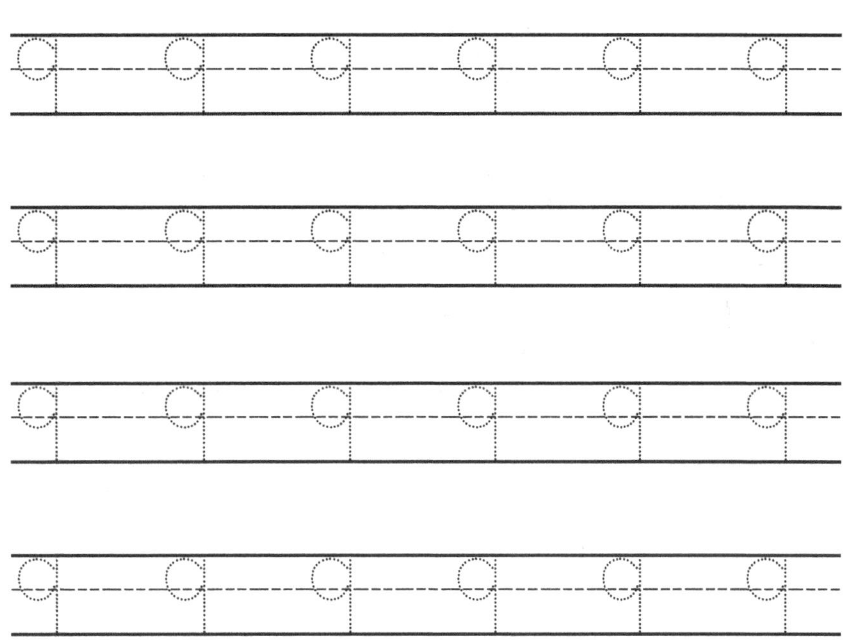

Trace the word Nine

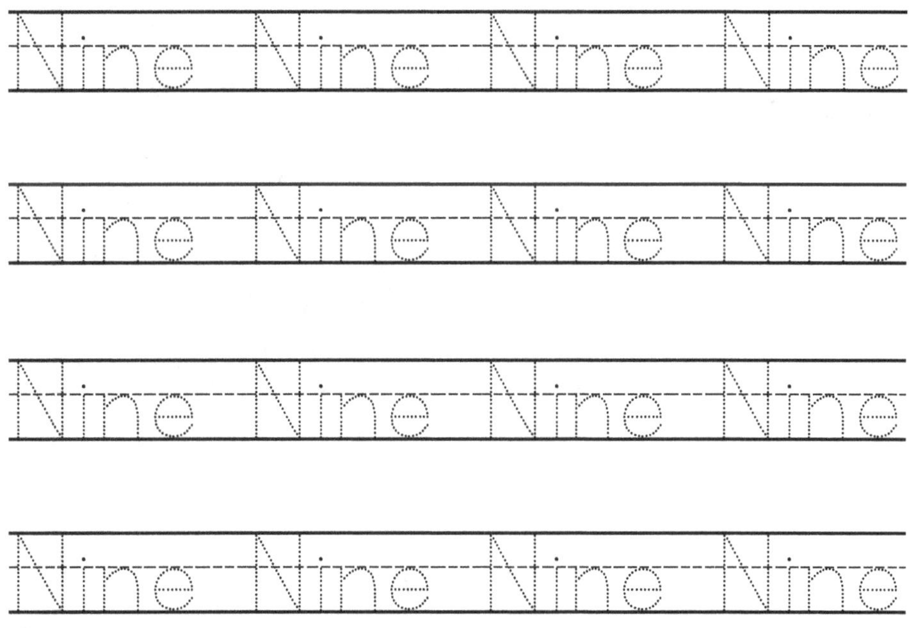

9

Nine

Color nine Spikes of wheat

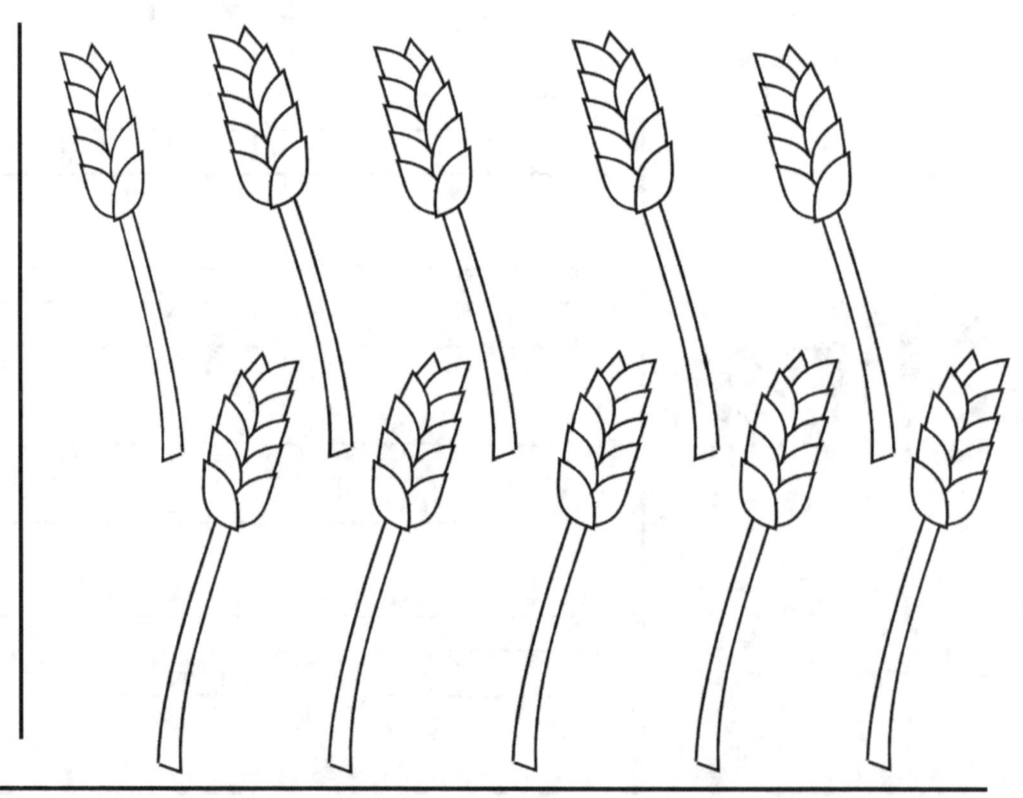

10

Trace the Number 10

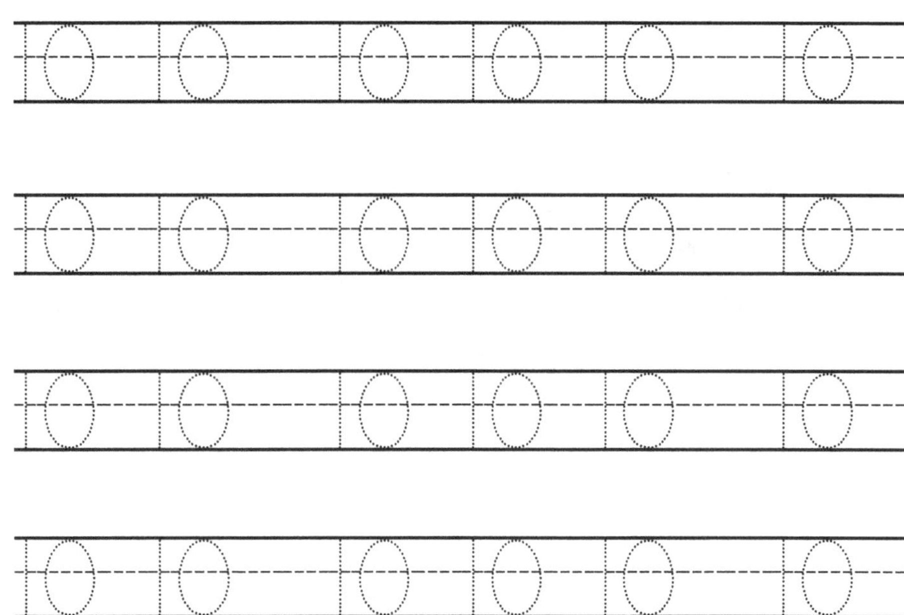

Ten

Trace the word Ten

Write Number 10

10 - - - - - - - - - - -

10 - - - - - - - - - - -

10 - - - - - - - - - - -

10 - - - - - - - - - - -

Ten

Color Ten Cherries

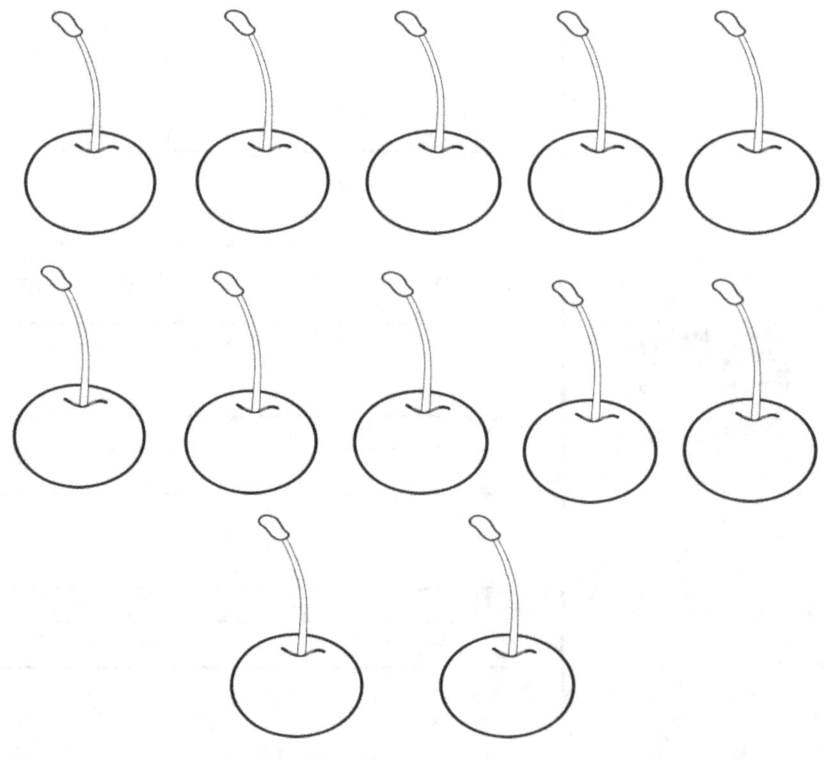